G000123164

A BOOT UP

BUTTERMERE AND CRUMMOCK WATER

Keith Wood

First published in Great Britain in 2009

British Library Cataloguing-in-Publication Data
A CIP record for this title is available from the British Library

ISBN 978 1 906887 30 8

PiXZ Books
Halsgrove House, Ryelands Industrial Estate,
Bagley Road, Wellington, Somerset TA21 9PZ
Tel: 01823 653777
Fax: 01823 216796
email: sales@halsgrove.com

An imprint of Halstar Ltd, part of the Halsgrove group of companies
Information on all Halsgrove titles is available at: www.halsgrove.com

Printed and bound by Grafiche Flaminia, Italy

Contents

How to use this book

The twin lakes of Buttermere and Crummock Water are situated at the bottom of a steep sided valley surrounded by a terrific array of high peaks. Formed at the end of the last ice age by glacial action, the valley starts at the top of Honister Pass and descends steeply down the pass to the farm at Gatesgarth. Filling the bottom of the valley is the lake of Buttermere itself followed by the hamlet of Buttermere consisting of a couple of farms, inns and small church. Crummock Water follows leading to Kirkstile with Loweswater beyond before finally heading out to the Solway Firth.

Originally a single sheet of water Buttermere became separated from Crummock Water with the build up of debris and silt brought down by the side valley that we know today as Newlands Pass. This tight valley surrounded by high peaks makes for a walkers' paradise and is justifiably popular with today's visitors, although the steep sides and some of the highest peaks mean that they are outside the scope of this book of leisure walks. I've chosen a selection of walks suitable for all ages and abilities graded from Easy to More-Challenging. The Easy walks are mostly short walks in the valley bottom, moving on to those graded fair which are either longer in distance or include some ascent with those graded More Challenging offering a true taste of Lake District fell walking ascending to some of the higher peaks surrounding the lakes.

The nature of the geography means that human habitation is extremely sparse and likewise the opportunity for refreshment and facilities are limited outside the two "main" centres of Buttermere and Kirkstile — also known as Loweswater. Whilst both have places of worship neither are really large enough to be called villages — hamlets would be a more appropriate term. However Buttermere has a couple of hotels (with bars and restaurants open to non residents) and two cafés and Kirkstile has the well known Kirkstile Inn.

All ten walks are covered by the Ordnance Survey Explorer Map OL4: The English Lakes, North-Western area, and Harvey's Lakeland West and Lakeland Central Maps. The maps in this book are only an outline version of each walk and the detail provided by the OS maps puts each route in context.

Every year tens of thousands of visitors enjoy the fells with the vast majority coming to no harm. However there are many cases each year where walkers are injured, get lost or find themselves in some other kind difficulty requiring the assistance of the Mountain Rescue Services. A few simple precautions should help avoid any problems:

• If you are unsure about your fitness start with the walks graded Easy and work your way up to More Challenging.
• Wear suitable footwear — properly fitted walking boots are recommended for all the walks.
• Take suitable clothing; the weather in the Lake District can change very quickly, take a waterproof and extra warm layers to wear.
• Take plenty to eat and drink en route, dehydration and lack of nourishment can lead to fatigue and mistakes being made.
• An outline map illustrates each walk but it is recommended that a complete map is taken.
• Inform someone of your planned route and expected return time.
• Check the weather forecast in advance and only take to the more challenging routes on clear days.
• And finally keep to the paths and watch where you are putting your feet — most accidents are caused by careless slips!

Reflections in Buttermere

Useful websites:

Lake District National Park

www.lake-district.gov.uk

National Trust

www.nationaltrust.org.uk

Friends of the Lake District

www.fld.org.uk

Cumbria Tourist Board

www.cumbria-the-lake-district.co.uk

Cumbria Tourism

www.golakes.co.uk

Lake District Outdoors

www.lakedistrictoutdoors.co.uk

Traveline – Public Transport Information

www.traveline.org.uk

Keith Wood Photography

www.keithwoodphotography.co.uk

Mellbreak from Buttermere

Key to Symbols Used

Level of difficulty:
Easy
Moderate
More Challenging 🐾🐾🐾

Map symbols:

🚗	Park & start
—	Tarred Road
- - -	Footpath
- - -	Walk Footpath
■	Building
+	Church
▲	Triangulation pillar or other landmark
🚻	WC
🍴	Refreshments
🍺	Pub

Brackenthwaite

Loweswater

9 10 8

LOWESWATER FELL

CRUMMOCK WATER

DERWENT FELLS

7

Buttermere 1

5 6

BUTTERMERE FELL

BUTTERMERE

Gatesgarth

2 3

Honister Pass

4

ENNERDALE WATER

Walk Locations

St James's Church, Buttermere

6

1 High Snockrigg

The ideal place to start with a view of the whole valley

Level:
Length: 1¼miles (2km)
Ascent: 630 feet (190m)
Terrain: Steep climb followed by walk around the edge of Buttermere Moss to the high point
Park and start: Plenty of off road parking available at the top of Newlands Hause
Start ref: GR 192 177
Info: Refreshments available down in Buttermere

Whilst being the shortest walk in the book it may not be the easiest consisting of a short steep climb and descent at either end of the walk. But it does make the ideal first walk taking you to a viewpoint from which all the other walks in the book can be viewed! From the highest point the whole of the valley from Honister Pass, full length views of Buttermere and Crummock Water and the extension of the valley along Loweswater to the Solway Firth and the hills of Scotland beyond can be seen. Try and save this one for a clear day – High Snockrigg and Buttermere Moss are not places to be in the mist!

Whilst I'm obviously a keen walker I stand by the adage of minimum effort for maximum impact. This walk certainly follows that rule by starting from the car at Newlands Hause the highest point between the Newlands and Buttermere Valleys at some 1100 feet above sea level meaning that there is only 600 feet of climbing necessary to reach the high point of 1700 feet, considerably less effort than starting down at Buttermere itself.

Map labels:
B5289
Newlands Hause
Buttermere
High Snockrigg
Buttermere Moss
Goat Crag
BUTTERMERE
B5289
1 2 3

1 Park at the top of the pass separating the Newlands Valley and Buttermere at Newlands Hause where there is plenty of car parking space on either side of the road. The walk heads up High Snockrigg on a narrow path directly up the hillside on the same side of the road as the waterfall which crashes down from above. Initially walking on smooth short cropped grass, the path

Eel Crags from the ascent

immediately starts to rise and quickly a narrow stony path materialises. Head straight up the fellside with the path alternating between a stony surface and grass; steeply rising above the pass. Whilst pausing to regain your breath take a look behind for a full length view along Newlands Valley towards Blencathra with the Pennines in the distance. Just on the other side of the road is the impressive ridge of Whiteless Pike to Wandope, Eel Crags and Sail. The path continues to zig zag up the fellside on this short sharp ascent onto the plateau above.

2 After the short 20 minute climb the path emerges from the top of a narrow gulley onto the open moor of High Snockrigg with the full height of Robinson to the front left. Another great place to pause and enjoy the views. Popping up from the gulley pick up a faint path heading across the moorland to the right, continuing to now gently rise. Keep to the faint but clear enough path which gently meanders towards the highest point of High Snockrigg to overlook Buttermere. As you're walking along here there is an impressive view to the left over the wet bog of Buttermere Moss and the giant pudding bowl shape of Great Gable can be seen on the horizon. Next into sight down to the right is Crummock Water, the view being split by the ridge of Rannerdale Knotts with Mellbreak behind and then along to Loweswater with the Solway and Scotland in the distance. Just continue following the path which

Rannerdale Knotts and Crummock Water from High Snockrigg

Buttermere Moss was once used as a source of peat for the fires of the village. Peat is one of nature's most efficient natural stores of carbon. Because of the wet, airless, and acidic conditions in a healthy bog, there is limited decomposition releasing carbon into the atmosphere – the peat acting as a carbon reservoir.

meanders around the front edge of High Snockrigg to reach the highest point itself. Barely quarter of an hour after reaching the plateau the grassy summit at the front of High Snockrigg is reached marked by a small cairn of stones. Just walk a few more paces forward to get the magnificent view of the whole of Buttermere with the imposing wall of Red Pike, High Stile and High Crag directly ahead; the trio of fells which tower over Buttermere. Looking to the left to the head of the lake Fleetwith Pike rises majestically with the little rocky fell of Haystacks in the middle ground. To the right the view continues along Crummock Water and beyond to Loweswater, and further round to the right the great mass of Grasmoor with the ridge from Whiteless Pike to Sail. Directly behind is the summit of Robinson across the boggy ground of Buttermere Moss.

(3) Having taken in the views all that remains is to retrace your steps back to the top of the gulley across the moorland and then to carefully make your way down the steep slope to the start point below. Possibly needing to use your hands and bottom as a break where required. Enjoy the panoramic views as you return across the high ground around Buttermere Moss. Upon returning to the Hause it's a worthwhile short detour to go and inspect the impressive waterfall coming down from Robinson.

Sunset on Crummock Water

2 Fleetwith Pike

A real mountain climb to a stunning viewpoint

Fleetwith Pike dominates the Buttermere Valley. From anywhere around the lake it makes an imposing spectacle, rising from the valley floor its ridge ascends skywards as straight as the flight of an arrow. Anyone driving down Honister Pass should also realise that the crags to the left are all part of Fleetwith Pike. Plundered for its slate over the years by mining activity, its insides are riddled with tunnels and caverns. But it is to the imposing ridge that this walk belongs making it one of the "More Challenging" walks in the collection but one which is well worth the effort for the commanding views from anywhere along the ridge.

289

Level: 🐾 🐾 🐾
Length: 3½ miles (5km)
Ascent: 1825 feet (550m)
Terrain: A long steep climb, a dart across country and a steady descent on clear paths
Park and start: Car park at Gatesgarth Farm
Start ref: GR 196 149
Info: Refreshments available at Honister Mine and in Buttermere

Fleetwith Pike from Warnscale Bottom

11

Fleetwith Pike across Buttermere

1 Starting from the car park at Gatesgarth Farm at the foot of Honister Pass, walk a short way up the road between a couple of buildings and at a finger post on the right take the Public Footpath towards Fleetwith Pike where the ascent commences immediately. The path passes the white Memorial Cross to Fanny Mercer, "accidentally killed in 1887", on a set of carefully graduated zig zags on a repaired section of path. The crest of the ridge is soon reached and from here the path follows the line of the ridge steeply gaining height all the way to the summit. There are a couple of sections where the path becomes even steeper where it's necessary to use your hands to lever yourself over rocks. For the entire climb there are the most incredible

Looking down the ridge

retrospective views along the Buttermere Valley, to Crummock Water, Mellbreak and across the Solway to Scotland; these give plenty of excuses to pause for a much needed breather on the ascent. All of a sudden the summit is reached with the view to the south and east opening up.

2 From the summit of Fleetwith Pike take the initially faint trod heading down towards the remains of Dubbs Quarry with its heaps of waste grey slate. The path rapidly becomes clearer on the ground, and gently loses height through the heather and bilberry clad slopes.

3 At Dubbs Quarry make your way through the remains of the long abandoned slate mine to pick up the old tramway between the quarry and Honister Pass. Take care when picking your way between the old workings; silence now rules in a place that must have been noisy and dusty in its hey day. Pass Dubbs Hut, a restored mine building now used as a camping barn or bothy, which although providing only the most basic of accommodation still offers welcome relief in bad weather. From the hut head down to a junction of paths, near the source of Warnscale Beck (spelt Wharnscale on Harvey's Maps).

4 Coming down from Dubbs Quarry at the crossroads of paths at Warnscale Beck take the path heading down on the right side of the beck. This rocky path descends

Geologists believe that the slate was originally deposited here as volcanic ash, which settled in water and was then subjected to immense pressures. Honister green slate is thicker and stronger than Welsh slate – and could be the strongest in the world, with 55 Kg weight to the square metre.

initially heading towards the cliffs of Green Crag with the beck on the left, before swinging around to the right and continues to descend towards Warnscale Bottom along the flank of Fleetwith Pike. The path starts to level out as the valley bottom is reached and a large cairn of stones is passed

Fleetwith Pike

The view from the top of Warnscale Beck

immediately followed by a ruined building on the right. The path now starts to flatten out as it proceeds along Warnscale Bottom along the base of Fleetwith Pike. The views remain stunning even at this low level as you near the end of the walk, with High Crag dominating the foreground and further along Buttermere comes back into sight with Mellbreak beyond. The path passes a plantation of Scots Pines on the left and the white boathouse at the end of Buttermere comes into view. Walking along the level, this wide stony track swings around to the right around the end of the Pike. The track meets up with the road down from Honister Pass and all that remains is to turn left, passing between the buildings back to the start point.

3 Haystacks

A climb to the top of the favourite fell of the most famous fellwalker Alfred Wainwright

This magnificent round explores some of the favourite places of Alfred Wainwright, the master fellwalker. From Gatesgarth Farm the route climbs up beside Warnscale Beck before passing Innominate Tarn, the final resting place of the great man's ashes and visiting Haystacks, his favourite summit.   Whilst not quite reaching the 2000 feet mark often defined as the height required to be recognised as a mountain (Haystacks is actually 1958 feet or 597m high) Wainwright described Haystacks as standing "unabashed and unashamed in the midst of a circle of much loftier fells, like a shaggy terrier in the company of foxhounds".

From previous visits on murky days, I must confess to having not been able to understand what the fuss was all about; however visiting on a fine summer's day, I have to agree; Haystacks is a wonderful place, a dwarf among giants making for a great viewing platform of the western fells and Innominate Tarn on a quiet day is an idyllic location.

Level: 🐾 🐾 🐾
Length: 4¾miles (7.6km)
Ascent: 1900 feet (575m)
Terrain: Good paths throughout.
Park and start: Car park at Gatesgarth Farm
Start ref: GR 196 149
Info: Refreshments available at Honister Mine and in Buttermere

---

Gatesgarth Farm

Gatesgarthdale Beck

1

Warnscale Beck

Low Raven Crag

High Raven Crag

Fleetwith Pike

Dubbs Quarry

2

Old Tramway

Black Beck

Green Crag

Dubbs Bottom

5

Haystacks

4

3

Innominate Tarn

Black Beck Tarn

① Park at the car park opposite Gatesgarth Farm on the bank of Gatesgarthdale Beck at the foot of Honister Pass. Leave the car park to turn left to walk up the road. Pass a couple of buildings on either side of the road and immediately a track heads off to the right signed Public Bridleway. Take the Bridleway ignoring the Public Footpath which heads up Fleetwith Pike — save that one for another day. The track heads around the base of Fleetwith Pike and Haystacks is directly to the front walking on the level on this loose surfaced track with the marsh and fields of Warnscale Bottom just below. The track gradually swings around to the left as it passes a plantation of spindly and tall Scots Pines on the right. The further you walk along the more intimidating the climb ahead appears but from here the clear zig zag path can be seen making its way at an acceptable incline up the face of the fell. The path just goes deeper along Warnscale Bottom with crags above on three sides. As the end of the valley is approached simply stay on the main path as it starts to ascend the fellside keeping to the left. Ignore the faint path off to the right across the beck. Pass a ruined building on the left and a large cairn of stones which marks the start of the

Haystacks

real ascent; just keep following the path as it initially gently rises up the sides of Fleetwith Pike before swinging around to the right across the head of the valley. Beneath the buttress of Green Crag the path swings back around to the left and continues to rise before emerging at a crossroads of paths on the edge of Dubbs Bottom.

(2) Cross the beck and heading to the right continue on the well worn path around the ridge leading to Haystacks. The path which has undergone erosion repair in places starts to gain some of the previously lost height. Enjoy the delights of the soggy hinterland of Haystacks passing by Blackbeck Tarn with Great Gable looming in the distance.

Haystacks and High Crag from the top of Warnscale Beck

Blackbeck Tarn

Innominate Tarn

marking the top of the fell with a small tarn in between. From the summit there is a full length view down Ennerdale with Pillar and High Crag making an imposing spectacle. Continue over the top of Haystacks to pick up a clear path down to the top of Scarth Gap Pass. The track is steep

Innominate Tarn is a small tarn near the summit of Haystacks. It is the location of the ashes of Alfred Wainwright. The modern name replaces the earlier 'Loaf Tarn', which accurately describes the lumps of peat surrounded by the waters of the tarn, looking like pieces of risen dough.

 The path continues on to Innominate Tarn. The main track passes Innominate Tarn with its small islands which on a sunny summer's day make for an idyllic location; you can easily see why Wainwright was attracted to it. From the tarn all that remains is a short climb up to the summit of Haystacks.

4 There are two cairns of indistinguishable height difference

and rocky in places requiring the occasional use of hands (and bottom) for safe descent.

5 The crossroads of paths marking the top of Scarth Gap Pass is quickly reached; turn right to descend to Buttermere. About halfway down the view improves to include the full length of Buttermere and across to Fleetwith Pike where you can appreciate the steepness of the climb earlier in the day.

6 Upon reaching the lakeshore footpath, it's a simple matter of following the path along the lakeshore around the head of the lake on the wide path straight back to Gatesgarth Farm.

High Crag above Scarth Gap

4 Grey Knotts and Brandreth

*A walk over two 2000 footers returning along
a smugglers route.*

Level: 🐾 🐾
Length: 3½miles (5.6km)
Ascent: 1350 feet (410m)
Terrain: A stiff climb followed by easy walking on well used high mountain paths
Park and start: National Trust car park at top of Honister Pass
Start ref: GR 225 135
Info: Refreshments available at Honister Mine www.honister-slate-mine.co.uk

This walk gives the opportunity of walking in the heart of the high mountains of Lakeland, giving spectacular views, but avoiding most of the climbing by starting at the high point of Honister Pass. The walk starts with a stiff climb up to the summit of Grey Knotts at 697m or 2287' where an outstanding full panoramic view dramatically comes into sight on reaching the summit. A gentle stroll to the summit of Brandreth, at 2344' (715m) the highest point on the route follows, where it is worthwhile stopping to enjoy some classic views of Pillar, Kirk Fell and the two Gables, separated by Windy Gap.

The return route follows the infamous Moses Trod, reputedly named after a Honister quarryman who smuggled illegally distilled whisky along the track into Wasdale. Walking along Moses Trod delivers full length views of Buttermere and Crummock Water, before reaching the ruined Drum House on the old tramway back down to Honister.

289

Gatesgarthdale Beck

🧭 E

🚌 Honister Pass

1

way 5

ottom

Plumbago Mines (disused)

Grey Knotts 2   Raven Crag

3 **Brandreth**

1 From the car park you can clearly see the path heading up the fellside beside a wire fence. Pass through the slate mine compound; there is a stile at the bottom corner of the compound that needs crossing to get to the path. The hard work starts immediately with most of the height of the day to be gained right at the start of the walk. The path climbs steeply on a well pitched path straight up the fellside alongside the wire fence. Halfway up, the path enters a craggy section, starting with a minor scramble up a 10' rock slab before returning to the pitched path. The path now zig zags through the crags before coming to a narrow gulley where a 4 foot block is climbed needing hands and feet before returning to the path once again next to the

Honister Crag and Pass

Great Gable from Brandreth

wire fence. The path continues up towards the summit of Grey Knotts with the incline now much gentler. Keep next to the wire fence, stopping to enjoy the views which just get better and better the more height is gained. As the summit comes into view, you reach a stile over the fence, cross the stile and follow the well defined trod to the summit. A final scramble on the highest rocky outcrop brings you onto the summit with a cairn indicating the highest point of 2287ft.

2 Upon reaching the summit on a clear day a dramatic full 360 degree panorama opens out.

From Grey Knotts the route to Brandreth is a simple stroll heading on a line between Great Gable and Kirk Fell. A faint path meanders between rocks and a few pools of water for the half mile to the summit of Brandreth directly in front.

There are three distinct high points, two adorned with a single fence post, but the true summit is the third and furthest away with a cairn and a number of fence posts. Take a few moments at the summit to appreciate the majesty of Great Gable dominating the scene to the front, with the Wastwater Screes in the distance.

High Crag and Buttermere from Moses Trod

3 From the summit take a faint path towards Great Gable and a lonely fence post. Keep on this path until it is crossed by another clear and cairned path from left to right. Turning right join this new path and head along the line of cairns in the direction of Ennerdale. Continue along the cairned route, which gradually swings round towards Buttermere, gently losing height.

4 The path swings round again to face Dale Head and Honister. Now walking along Moses Trod, a typical high level Lakeland Path, there are continuous fine views to the left down the Buttermere Valley and along to Crummock Water.

Buttermere and Crummock Water
from Moses Trod

Pillar from Brandreth

After almost three centuries of production slate mining at Honister ceased in 1986. Laying idle for ten years the mine reopened and is now a highly successful enterprise. It is preserving and applying age old skills such as docking, riving and dressing, and it has given rise to an extremely popular visitor attraction.

(5) As the path nears the old tramway it passes a series of huge cairns and across some wet ground. On reaching the ruined buildings of what was once the Winding House for the Honister Mine tramway for transporting slate down to the mine, you now reach the main path from Honister to Buttermere. Turn right, steeply descending down to Honister Mine along the route of the disused slate tramway.

At the foot of the tramway, pass a slate constructed donation box for Cockermouth Mountain Rescue. Please make a donation, you never know when you may need them!! Finally cross through the yard of the Slate Mine, which is well worth a visit and then back to the car.

5 **Circuit of Buttermere**

Join the crowds and enjoy one of the Lake District's most popular walks

The circuit of Buttermere must be one of the most popular walks in the area and has appeared in numerous collections of walks — judging by my book shelves at any rate! Nevertheless that shouldn't discount it from being included in this collection of leisure walks around Buttermere and Crummock Water. It is popular because it is so special; relatively short on good paths which are on the level throughout and with superb scenery and views all the way round. It's suitable for all ages in all seasons and taking around a couple of hours can even be done as a summer evening's stroll. The biggest decision is whether to go around clockwise or anticlockwise, I've decided to describe the route anticlockwise which is my personal favourite.

Level: 🐾
Length: 4½miles (7.2km)
Ascent: Negligible
Terrain: Clear paths on the level throughout
Park and start: LDNP car park in Buttermere
Start ref: GR 175 169
Info: Refreshments at Syke House Farm, the Bridge Hotel, the Fish Hotel, Croft House Café.

Reflections in Buttermere

Map labels:
1 Buttermere
7
Goat Crag
2
6
B5289
Burtness Wood
BUTTERMERE
5
Comb Beck
Gatesgarth
4
3
Low Raven Crag
Warnscale Beck

N
W E
S

Whiteless Pike across Buttermere

1. Park in the LDNP car park behind the Fish Hotel, walk back around the front of the hotel to pick up the Public Bridleway to Buttermere Lake and Scale Bridge along a farm track. Walk down the quiet lane heading towards the spectacular Sour Milk Gill pouring down the mountainside from Red Pike. Approaching the lake pass through a gate, where the path splits but it does not matter which you take as both end up at the same point in about 100yds.

Cross the wooden footbridge over the outflow from Buttermere and almost immediately over another footbridge over Sour Milk Gill as its flows into the lake.

2. Pass through a wooden gate and then take the lower of the two paths on the left to take the lakeshore path. Walking along the lower edge of Burtness Wood with its mixed woodland the path forks again take the Permitted Path along the lakeshore. About half way along pass into an area of immature beech trees to arrive at a beautiful little bay where the view opens out across the lake. The path forks again; both meet at the same point a bit further along. Take either the higher path through the trees or my preference the path which hugs the lake for the better views.

Pass through a wooden gate in a drystone wall to leave the woods with High Crag and Comb Beck tumbling down the fellside to the right. Cross the wooden footbridge over Comb Beck. The path approaches the head of the lake with a magnificent view of Fleetwith Pike and Haystacks straight ahead. As the path forks again the path to the right leads up to Scarth Gap and Haystacks; keep to the lower left hand fork approaching the end of the lake.

3 As the end of the lake is reached continue through the gate to the left and over the bridge spanning Warnscale Beck. Walk along the wide flat path at the head of the lake beneath Fleetwith Pike heading towards Gatesgarth with great views

High Stile across Buttermere

Mary Robinson, the 'Maid of Buttermere', was the young daughter of the landlord of the Fish Inn, who gained 'celebrity status' in the late 18th century for her innocent beauty. Unfortunately she fell victim to the charms of a notorious fraudster and bigamist, who was hanged for his crimes in Carlisle in 1803.

to the left looking along the full length of the lake back towards Buttermere village with Mellbreak and Rannerdale Knotts in the distance.

Pass the Cockermouth Mountain Rescue post at Gatesgarth Farm and follow the Public Bridleway through the farm beside Gatesgarthdale Beck to emerge at the Buttermere to Honister road.

4 Turn left to walk along this unavoidable stretch of road. Keep your eyes and ears open on this sometimes busy road. After a while the lakeshore is reached whilst still walking beside the road.

5 Approaching some spiky gorse bushes the path heads away from the road hugging the lake shore. Passing a rocky outcrop the path swings out into the lake towards a solitary ash tree on the promontory that juts into the lake. Walk along the grey slate beach to approach a stand of Scots pines. Passing the pine trees cross over a footbridge where the path

starts to climb round a rocky outcrop rising just above the lake with oak trees all around. Exposed tree roots and bare rock require care on this stretch of the route.

Reflections in Buttermere

6 The path arrives at the entrance to Hassness Tunnel cut through the rock to allow the path to continue. The tunnel is usually wet and, for taller walkers, mind your head!! Exiting the tunnel, a wooden gate gives access to the shoreline path with well spaced trees and level grass area. The path undulates along the eastern shoreline through light deciduous woodland and passes through a series of gated wire fences on this section.

7 As the shoreline at the foot of the lake is reached pass through a kissing gate and head away from the lake straight towards

Entrance to Hassness Tunnel

Buttermere village. Pass through another kissing gate and the path follows the field boundary; follow the clearly signed path around the fields to Buttermere village. Join the stone surfaced farm track into Syke Farm; pass between the farm buildings and join the road in front of the Bridge Hotel and return to the car.

Western shore of Buttermere

6 Great Borne and Starling Dodd

The most challenging walk in the collection with views into Ennerdale

To avoid the crowds why not try something a little different and head to a couple of the less fashionable fells instead. Great Borne and Starling Dodd are the northerly extension of the High Style and Red Pike ridge which towers over Buttermere. The walk takes us around the back of Buttermere and Crummock Water to visit Scale Force – Lakeland's highest waterfall – before exploring the hidden reaches of Mosedale rising to visit Floutern Tarn before climbing steeply to the twin summits of Great Borne and Starling Dodd. It might not attract the crowds but this walk certainly is a crowd pleaser with

Level: 🥾 🥾 🥾
Length: 9¼miles (15km)
Ascent: 2600 ft in total (790m)
Terrain: Some challenging walking over rocky paths, route is clear throughout.
Park and start: LDNP car park, Buttermere
Start ref: GR 175 170
Info: Toilets and refreshments in Buttermere

some great views and also the opportunity to see some old favourites from different angles.

Scale Bridge

Grasmoor across Crummock Water

1 Park in the LDNP car park in Buttermere, just behind the Fish Hotel. Alternatively there is the National Trust car park a little further on, but that will add another ½ mile to the total journey length. Start by heading down the Public Bridleway to Buttermere Lake and Scale Bridge. Take the first track to the right signed to Scale Bridge and Scale Force. At the end of the lane walk besides Buttermere Dubbs, the short stretch of water flowing between Buttermere and Crummock Water, before crossing over Scale Bridge. Turn right at the other side of the bridge onto the clear path to Scale Force and Crummock Water. At a fork in the path take the upper left hand path to shortly cross a wooden footbridge over a stream. Continue on the stony path, past a couple of holly trees and at a large pile of stones take the faint trod up to the left heading towards the intake wall and then swing around to the right at a higher level to pick up a clear path marked by cairns. Follow this boulder-strewn path heading to Scale Force. The path eventually swings around to the left and the going gets easier with Scale Beck below. The next stage of the journey past Scale Force up to Floutern Pass can be seen in the foreground. Pass through a kissing gate through a wall and below you'll see the red stained wooden footbridge over Scale Beck. Take time to explore the lower regions of Scale Force, Lakeland's highest waterfall, before continuing the journey.

2 Cross the wooden footbridge and continue on the clear path rising gently towards Mosedale with the top of Hen Comb coming into view. As the ground levels off the great wet morass at the head of Mosedale opens out with Floutern Crag and Steel Brow ahead; fortunately the path avoids the worst of the bog. Keep to the clear path around the head of Mosedale. Pass a large sheepfold and continue along through another dry boulder field — dry

Floutern Tarn

across the top of the pass the scene opens out to the west to the Irish Sea and a first glimpse of Ennerdale.

 From the top of the pass the next section of the journey up Steel Brow to Great Borne looks fearsomely steep following the line of the fence straight up. Go up the left side of the fence to be able to get the best views looking back down onto Floutern Tarn. First you have to negoti-ate your way around a boggy area to reach the start of the climb. Height is rapidly gained and the view down to Floutern Tarn is worth a minor detour away from the fence. Just when you think the climb will never end the path levels off and swings around towards the boulder-strewn summit of Great Borne. The OS survey column comes

for a few moments before the path heads into the boggy section across wet ground towards a wooden gate through a wire fence. Cutting across the corner of an enclosure, cross the wire fence again over a stile, and immediately cross the stream coming down from

Floutern Tarn to join the main path up to Floutern Pass. Turn left onto the main path up to the pass. The green path heads up to the tarn passing through another couple of fences and after a fairly steep climb Floutern Tarn is passed. As you reach the wire fence

into view on the opposite side of the fence which has to be carefully crossed at the most convenient point; a stile would be useful here. The summit just topping out at 2019' (616m) is marked by an OS column and adjacent wind shelter. For the best views down into Ennerdale you'll need to make a 100 yard detour across the rocky top towards Ennerdale to be able to look down onto the lake.

(4) To continue to Starling Dodd simply follow the clear path between the two fells, losing some height initially and passing a fenced off area. The path rises quite steeply up a grassy path for one last pull up to the top of Starling Dodd at 2085' (616m), the top of which is adorned with a metallic cairn of ancient fence posts.

Summit of Starling Dodd

(5) From Starling Dodd, thankfully it's downhill all the way. The red path coming up from Scale Force can be seen across the natural bowl to the north east. Head down to the col or depression between Starling Dodd and Red Pike. Pick a line away

from the path to take the best route possible to swing around the bowl on a level contour to join the path down to Scale Force. Paths do not exist here although you may be lucky enough to follow one of the may faint trods heading through the grass. The red path is quickly reached and descends towards Scale Beck. As the head of Scale Beck is reached the path swings around to the right continuing to lose height all the way. The path almost merges with the beck for a while and nearing the top of the falls care is needed where the path has been disturbed by a couple of landslips; the use of and hands and bottom are needed to safely negotiate the path at this point. The head of the ravine is reached where the water plunges down Scale Force and the path steeply descends on a series of well pitched zig zags down to the foot of the falls. And so all that remains upon reaching the foot of the falls is to retrace the steps of your outward journey all the way back to Buttermere.

Animal cruelty is not a modern phenomenon. A shocked traveller to the Lake District in the late 18th century described the 'sport' of throwing dogs from the top of Scale Force – a spectacle for the tourists! Fortunately, much to the relief of the local dog population this practice fell out of favour soon after.

Ennerdale

7 Rannerdale Knotts

*A walk up a hidden valley followed by a splendid ridge
for the best view of Crummock Water*

There are plenty of views of this small hill from other walks in this collection, whether it's looking across Crummock Water from Mellbreak or across Buttermere from the circuit of the lake.

But it's the view from High Snockrigg that shows the "hidden" valley of Rannerdale and gives an appreciation of the quality of the ridge itself that should give you the appetite for pulling on your boots and completing this short but high quality route. Whilst Rannerdale is famous for its show of bluebell blooms in May this walk is suitable for any time of year giving outstanding views from the ridge.

Level: 🐾 🐾
Length: 2½miles (4km)
Ascent: 1000 feet (300m)
Terrain: Gentle climb with steep descent
Park and start: Parking space at the foot of Rannerdale Knotts
Start ref: GR 163 184
Info: Toilets and refreshments in Buttermere

Map

B5289
Rannerdale Farm

2

Squat Beck

CRUMMOCK WATER

1

4
Rannerdale Knotts

Low Bank

3

B5289

Buttermere

Rannerdale Knotts

(1) Park in the small National Trust Parking Bay at the foot of Rannerdale Knotts. Head off through the back of the car park past the National Trust Rannerdale sign on the clear path running around the foot of Rannerdale Knotts with a well built drystone wall on the left. Grasmoor is right in front as you walk along the level on this first section. Pass through a kissing gate through a drystone wall coming down from the fellside. 50 yards further on the path starts to swing away from the wall around to the right continuing around the foot of the fell where the shapely pyramidal peak of Whiteless Pike comes clearly into view.

Continue on the path beneath the crags of Rannerdale, the waters of Squat Beck are now in the valley bottom to the left. If they are in season the bluebell blooms are concentrated on the opposite bank of the beck. Continue walking up the valley gaining some height on the right hand bank of the beck.

(2) A wooden footbridge crosses over the beck giving access to the opposite bank to inspect the bluebells. Continue on the right bank and pass through a gate through the drystone wall and continue on the clear and stony path up the valley with Whiteless Pike on the left. The beck gradually reduces in size to a trickle and after gaining some height the path flattens off as you walk along the edge of the wide bowl between Whiteless Pike and Rannerdale Knotts. Keep to the clear path walking along the secluded valley

Rannerdale Bluebell

of Rannerdale, and as the intake wall is left behind the path starts to gently rise again towards the hause which gives easy access to the ridge of Rannerdale Knotts. The path passes over the beck and continues gently rising up the valley with High Snockrigg in sight above the hause. As height is gained pause for a look back down the valley towards Crummock Water. Ignore the path to the right onto the ridge as you near the top of the valley; keep straight on the main path towards the house.

3   The view opens up as you meet the path down from

Whiteless Pike. Take the time to look down upon the village of Buttermere and the lake. Double back on yourself to pick up the grassy path along the top of the ridge of Rannerdale Knotts. After a short climb over the green turf the full length along the ridge comes into view. Simply follow the green

path along the top of the ridge, enjoying the magnificent views as you follow the ridge along. After a steep-ish climb, about a third of the way along the ridge a grassy plateau is reached which makes for another great viewing station before dropping down a little and then rising again towards the rocky peak. A final little scramble up a rocky knoll leads to the highest part of the ridge topped with three outcrops, the third and furthest along being the true top. Notice the vertical rock strata indicating some massive geological upheaval in the past. Pause to enjoy the magnificent panoramic view.

4   From the top it's clear that it's a steep descent from the top straight down to the valley

Looking along the ridge

Grasmoor from the summit of Rannerdale Knotts

below. Initially keep heading along the ridge, immediately losing height down a repaired path. Those with short legs may need the odd hand! Follow the rocky path and just before a crag blocks the way the path turns down to the left and starts to descend towards Crummock Water

with Mellbreak straight ahead. Follow the mostly green path steeply down the flank of Rannerdale Knotts. The path descends steeply down a gulley on a stepped path before continuing on grass again and swinging around to the right. Just before reaching the bottom walk onto the

outcrop jutting into the lake for a full length view of Crummock Water. Finally take the last few paces back down to the car park.

Rannerdale Knotts is said to be the site of a battle between the native Cumbrians and the invading Normans in the early 12th century. Nicholas Size, local historian and innkeeper of the Bridge Hotel, Buttermere, published a book in the 1930s 'The Secret Valley' blending fact and fiction of the Cumbrians struggle to maintain their independence.

Crummock Water and Floutern Pass from the ridge

8 Lanthwaite Green

Trio of Lanthwaites – Lanthwaite Green, Lanthwaite Hill and Lanthwaite Wood

Level: 🥾
Length: 2½miles (4km)
Ascent: 500 feet (150m)
Terrain: Easy paths throughout, mostly on the level with one gentle climb
Park and start: Lanthwaite Green
Start ref: GR 158 208
Info: Refreshments at Buttermere or Kirkstile Inn

Whilst not quite the shortest this is definitely the easiest walk in this collection, but is none the worse for that. A gentle walk around the north eastern end of Crummock Water which is suitable for all the family looking for a short outing and would make an ideal summer evening stroll at the end of the day. Starting from Lanthwaite Green there is chance to get a closer look at the imposing bulk of Grasmoor, whilst further on the views are of Crummock Water and the visit to the top of Lanthwaite Hill presents one of the best views along Crummock Water with Mellbreak in the background. A walk along the top of Lanthwaite Wood completes the trio of Lanthwaites visited on the route.

Farmer's sign in Cumbrian dialect

Brackenthwaite
Whiteside
B5289
Lanthwaite Hill
Lanthwaite Gate
Liza Beck
Lanthwaite Wood
Lanthwaite Green Farm
Grasmoor
B5289

TEK CARE LAMBS ONT ROAD

47

Grasmoor above Liza Beck

1. Park in the good sized car park at the side of the farm at Lanthwaite Green. Cross over the road and follow the wide green track between the bracken heading towards the gill between Grasmoor and Whiteside. The path gently rises over this open common land. Ignore the path heading off up to the right to Grasmoor. Now the path starts to head into the gill where a wooden footbridge crossing the Liza Beck comes into view; head towards the footbridge and cross the beck over the footbridge onto the opposite bank.

2. Immediately turn left on the narrow trod which rises along the edge of the fellside between prickly gorse just above the beck. Approaching a large drystone-walled

Liza Beck

3 As the path comes in line with
a white building in the valley bottom, a wooden walker's gate through the wall comes into view, pass through the gate and down the steps into the field. Walk through the field keeping to the left of the enclosure towards the beck. Cross over a stream using stepping stones and in 50 yards pass through a gate and then over the wooden footbridge over Liza Beck. Pass through a small stand of trees and in

Gate down to road

enclosure veer to the right to walk around the top corner and then follow the path just above the wall, with the wall immediately on the left. There are good views of Low Fell and Fellbarrow to the front left with the hummock of Lanthwaite Hill in the foreground. The path forks at a rock; take the lower left hand fork to continue walking beside the drystone wall. This is easy walking on the level just above the intake wall.

The surface of Crummock Water is a couple of feet higher than the River Cocker flowing out of it. To accommodate this there is a weir, sluice gate, and a fish ladder allowing brown trout, charr, pike, perch, sea trout, and salmon, to access the lake.

another 20 yards through another gate onto the road. Cross straight over the road and through a gate on the opposite side signposted Public Footpath to Scale Hill. Follow the path through the field which swings to the left and passes by the whitewashed building of Pickett How. Keep going to the gate in the bottom corner of the field.

(4) Pass through into the next enclosure where the path continues on with the field boundary on your right. Passing a copse of oak trees on the left the drystone wall swings away to the right and the path continues heading straight on and starting to gently rise on a clear path heading towards bracken. Keep to this path gently rising across the field until a drystone wall at the far end is reached enclosing some trees; continue rising slightly more steeply beside the trees. The path emerges onto the slopes of Lanthwaite Hill (Brackenthwaite Hows on Ordnance Survey maps) with a great view straight ahead to Mellbreak. To get the best view take a minor detour up to the left onto the top of the hill, before returning to this junction of paths. Turn

right and in another 20 yards there is a wooden stile through the wall and into the top of the woods.

(5) Cross over the stile and enter the oak woodland. 20 yards into the woods a clear path branches off to the left, and initially loses a bit of height. This path follows the drystone wall along the top of the woods. Continue through the trees along this high level path with the wall on your left. There are views through the trees across to Kirkstile and the Loweswater Fells with Crummock Water seen below.

(6) At a crossroads of paths take the left path, pass through a gate and pick up the path heading back towards Grasmoor with

Across Crummock Water to Red Pike from Lanthwaite Green

Lanthwaite Green and the car park in sight. The path swings around to the right to pass through another gate and along an ancient enclosed lane between the fields.

(7) The path emerges through another gate onto the road. Turn right and all that remains is the short walk back along the road to the start, passing the buildings of Lanthwaite Gate. Walk over the cattle grid past the farm buildings of Lanthwaite Green to arrive back at the start.

Mellbreak from Lanthwaite Hill

9 Around Mellbreak

Not over but around Mellbreak and along the shore of Crummock Water

Level: 🥾 🥾

Length: 6½miles (10.5km)

Ascent: 1100 feet (330m)

Terrain: Mostly good clear paths with a couple of boggy sections

Park and start: Maggie's Bridge National Trust car park Loweswater

Start ref: GR 134 210

Info: Refreshments from Kirkstile Inn

This walk takes a break from the tradition of walking round a lake but instead takes a walk around a fell and is equally suitable for a fine dry day or wet day out. Walking around Mellbreak, with its twin summits, which dominates the western shoreline of Crummock Water first takes us through into the quiet hidden valley of Mosedale walking between our subject and the little known Loweswater fell of Hen Comb. En route we are able to take in the added treat of visiting the spectacular Scale Force, tucked away between the trees at the foot of Red Pike which with its 170 ft drop makes it Lakeland's highest waterfall. The return along the shoreline of Crummock Water allows panoramic views across the lake to Rannerdale and Grasmoor.

53

1 Leave the car park and walk back up the lane to the Loweswater road, turn right at the T junction and continue walking along the road heading towards Kirkstile. Take the next right to walk down towards the Kirkstile Inn.

2 From the Kirkstile Inn, take the road passing the front of the inn towards Kirkhead. There is a road sign there to help, signed in one direction "No Road to Lake", and "No through Road" which is the direction to take. The road crosses a bridge over Park Beck on the way to the farm buildings of Kirkgate. After passing through the farm the road turns into a green lane with dry stone walls on either side and Mellbreak starts to dominate the scene straight in front.

Mellbreak from Kirkstile

As the lane reaches a small stand of trees, come to a gate. Go through the gate, immediately turning right with a wall now on your right hand side. (Do not go straight on through the fire-break between the trees, which takes you on the route directly up Mellbreak). The lane rises gently uphill and as you reach the crest take a look to the right for a fine view of

Great Bourne across Mosedale

Loweswater and Darling Fell. The route now turns southwards and the wall is left behind, walking on a good track down Mosedale between Hen Comb and Mellbreak.

3 Halfway along the valley at a large broken-down cairn, the route forks. Take the path to the left heading slightly uphill away from the main track. Walking along this path parallel to the valley bottom you will pass Mosedale's lonely holly tree. About 300 yards past the holly tree the path becomes quite faint on the ground, but have faith and keep going straight on, heading to Red Pike passing a lonely metal gate serving no purpose, fenceless either side. About 150 yards past the lonely gate, the path splits, with the main track swinging around to the left, you take the track going straight on across some marshy ground until you meet a wire fence with a gate and stile. Go over the stile and follow the path

straight down the side of a wire fence to the valley bottom enjoying the sweeping views of the Buttermere Valley with Fleetwith Pike and Robinson.

4 At the valley bottom, join another path heading left towards Scale Force and Buttermere. Follow the good track down with Black Beck bubbling away to your right. Upon reaching a large flat rock the path splits; go right down to cross the beck and follow the path up through the bracken towards the bridge at Scale Force.

5 Take a break at Scale Force to inspect Lakeland's highest waterfall. From the bridge at Scale Force backtrack a few paces and take

the path between two iron fence posts heading down towards Crummock Water now with Scale Beck on the right. Walk down to where the two becks meet and cross a small bridge before continuing heading towards Crummock keeping the beck to your immediate right.

6 As you approach the lakeshore the path swings left along the shore in front of Mellbreak with classic views across Crummock Water to Rannerdale and Grasmoor. Continue along the lakeshore path which can be boggy in places in wet weather, making the detour onto the spit of Low Ling Crag jutting into the water and then continue along the lakeshore, past a small wind blasted Rowan Tree.

Scale Force

7 As you reach the foot of the lake the Loweswater Fells come back into sight. 200yds after crossing a broken wall, a complete wall is seen ahead, and a track heading up through the bracken to the left is reached. Take this track

Looking across Crummock Water

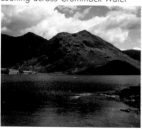

away from the lakeshore, which shortly reaches a good higher path heading towards the wall. As you reach the wall after a short gentle incline the path flattens out. Pause at the wall to take a last fine retrospective view along the full length of Crummock Water, with Haystacks in view at the end of the valley beyond Buttermere. The path now winds downhill with the wall to your right, to a fine stand of ancient oaks.

8 After passing through the wood with High Park Farm on the right you reach a wall and gate, go through gate, onto an old green lane. Pass the buildings of Lowpark to reach a surfaced lane and progress left over a bridge. After 150 yards, at the T junction turn left, along the road back to the Kirkstile Inn where you can now enjoy a well earned pint before retracing your steps along the lane back to Maggie's Bridge car park.

Grasmoor and Crummock Water from Scale Force

10 Loweswater

A gentle stroll around the third lake along the valley

It seems appropriate to complete this collection of walks along the Buttermere and Crummock Water Valley with a walk around the third lake along the valley: Loweswater. Situated just over a mile from the foot of Crummock Water, Loweswater has its own distinctive character and is also is a much quieter place to visit. It is surrounded by its own set of hills with Darling Fell and Low Fell to the north of the lake, whilst to the south Burnbank Fell, Carling Knott and Blake Fell dominate the scene. At nearly 100 feet higher than Crummock Water, the water from Loweswater actually flows into Crummock Water along Dubbs and Park Becks before flowing from Crummock Water along the River Cocker.

Level: 🐑
Length: 3½ miles (5.6km)
Ascent: 300 feet (90m)
Terrain: Mostly clear footpaths with some unavoidable road sections
Park and start: Maggie's Bridge National Trust car park Loweswater
Start ref: GR 134 210
Info: Refreshments available at Kirkstile Inn, Loweswater

Map

redale Place · ④ Waterend

Darling Fell

⑤

on Place

⑥

LOWESWATER

③ Crabtree

urnbank Fell

Watergate Farm

Dubbs Beck

②

🅿 ①

Loweswater (Kirkstile)

Kirkhead

Park Beck

N W E S

① Start from the National Trust Maggie's Bridge car park at the southern end of Loweswater by walking back up the narrow lane away from the lake up to the "main" road at the top of the lane.

② Coming to the top of the lane there is a good view to the right across to Grasmoor and a glimpse of Crummock Water. Reaching the main road turn left to head along this unavoidable stretch of road where Loweswater itself can be seen down below. Take care on this quiet stretch of road where it's wise to keep your eyes and ears open for any approaching traffic. Pass High Cross with its imposing gate posts and continue walking along the road. With Low Fell up to the right the road passes High

Thrushbank and Thrushbank dating from 1697. The road now drops towards the lake shore.

3 Just over Crabtree Beck a path drops down from the road to the left to follow the lakeshore path just below the road. It's easy walking through the trees along the eastern shore of the lake with good view across to Burnbank and Blake Fells on the opposite bank. Approaching the end of the lake a drystone wall bars any further progress by the shore. Head up the path beside the wall to regain the road and continue along the road again. The distinctive white buildings of Hudson Place come into view on the opposite bank. A path deviates away from the road again, passes by

a parking place before a final stretch along the road. The abundant lichen in the hedgerow indicates the good air quality in this western part of the Lake District.

4 Pass a large lay by with a telephone box and at the end of the lay by turn left through a kissing gate to head down the field with the signpost "Public Footpath Holme

Way signs along the route

Wood ½ mile". The path heads down the edge of the field with a stream on the right; half way down cross over the stream and over a stile into the next field and cutting off the corner of this field reach a wooden footbridge over a beck. Walk along the boardwalked section over the marsh at the end of the lake to arrive at a gate and the lane up to Hudson's Place. Through the gate and head left on the surfaced lane gently rising to Hudson's Place. Approaching the top of the lane there is good view of Darling Fell and the full length of Loweswater with Mellbreak prominent at the end of the lake. Carry on past Hudson Place signposted "Bridleway to Holme Wood".

Whiteside seen across Loweswater

 5 Pass the farm buildings where the lane swings around to the left through a six bar gate. Follow the slate "Footpath" sign which directs you down the now un-surfaced lane back towards the lake. There are great views as you walk down this walled lane. Climb over the stile at the bottom of the lane to gain the lakeshore track with open views down onto the lake.

6 Pass through the gate into Holme Wood on the track

through the trees. Almost immediately a narrow path veers away to the left away from the track – both meet up at the same point further along – but to follow the lake shore take this narrow path on the left. At the bothy the lakeshore path rejoins the main track through the woods and continues along the lakeshore. The track leaves the wood through a gate and goes through the meadows around Loweswater passing through Watergate Farm. Finally the wide unsurfaced farm track meanders through the meadows back to Maggie's Bridge.

Lichen in the hedgerow

The buoy in the lake is an automatic water quality monitoring station collecting data every minute of water and air temperature, wind speed and water quality. The results are being used to understand how the lake functions and to check the impact of various local land management actions.

Holme Wood Bothy

Carling Knott